KU-207-178

Let's Experiment with Science

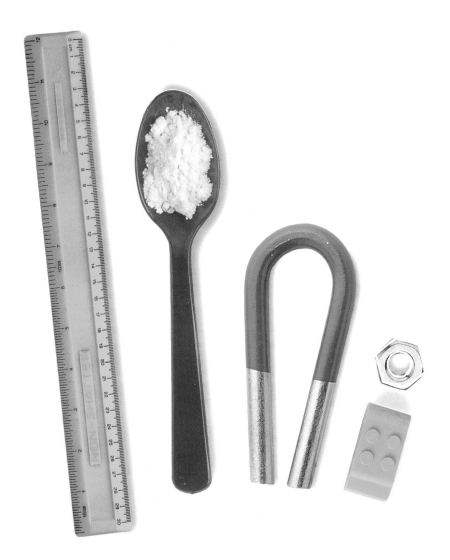

Let's Experiment with Science

JACK CHALLONER and ANGELA WILKES

DK

DORLING KINDERSLEY
London • New York • Stuttgart • Moscow

How to use this book

Let's Experiment with Science is full of interesting projects to try at home, from testing magnets to creating an incredible bottle volcano. Below are the points to look out for when using this book and a list of things to remember.

Equipment
Illustrated checklists show you which tools to have ready before you start a project.

The things you need
The materials to collect for each project are clearly shown to help you check that you have everything you need.

Step-by-step
Step-by-step photographs and clear instructions tell you exactly what to do at each stage of a project.

Things to remember

- Read through all the instructions and gather together everything you will need before you begin a project.

- Put on an apron, roll up your sleeves, and cover your work area with newspaper before you start.

- Follow the instructions carefully at each stage of the experiment and only do one thing at a time.

- Be very careful with sharp scissors. Do not use them unless there is an adult there to help you.

- Keep a record of each experiment or project and note down the results of your tests.

- When you have finished, put everything away, clean up any mess, and wash your hands.

A DORLING KINDERSLEY BOOK

Editor Fiona Campbell
Text Designer Caroline Potts
Managing Editor Jane Yorke
Managing Art Editor Chris Scollen
Production David Hyde
Photography Dave King and Mike Dunning
Illustrator Brian Delf

First published in Great Britain in 1996
by Dorling Kindersley Limited,
9 Henrietta Street,
London WC2E 8PS

Copyright © 1996 Dorling Kindersley Limited, London
Projects originally published in *My First Science Book*,
My First Green Book, and *My First Batteries and Magnets Book*
Copyright © 1990, 1991, 1992 Dorling Kindersley Limited, London

Visit us on the World Wide Web at http://www.dk.com

All rights reserved. No part of this publication may be reproduced, stored in a retrieval system, or transmitted in any form or by any means, electronic, mechanical, photocopying, recording, or otherwise without the prior written permission of the copyright owner.

A CIP catalogue record for this book is available from the British Library.

ISBN 0-7513-5520-8

Colour reproduction by Colourscan
Printed and bound in Italy by L.E.G.O.

CONTENTS

WATER FILTER

We expect clean water to drink whenever we turn on the tap. But because most of our drinking water comes from rivers, reservoirs, and under the ground, it starts off dirty and full of germs. It has run through rocks and soil, and can contain the wastes of animals and plants, and polluting chemicals. So the water that we use in our homes has to be specially cleaned at a waterworks to make it safe to drink before it reaches our taps. Try constructing this water filter, to find out how it is done.

A jug of water

Soil

You will need

Grass and leaves

EQUIPMENT

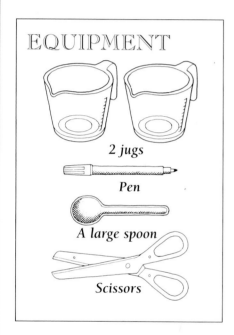

2 jugs

Pen

A large spoon

Scissors

Blotting paper

Gravel or small stones

Coarse sand

A clean flower pot

Making the water filter

1 Spoon some small amounts of soil, sand, gravel, grass, and leaves into the jug of water. Stir everything together.

2 Stand the flower pot on the blotting paper and draw around the base of the pot. Cut the circle out of the blotting paper.

3 Put the circle of blotting paper at the bottom of the flower pot. Half fill the pot with sand, then add a layer of gravel.

Using the water filter

Stand the flower-pot-filter on top of an empty jug. Slowly pour the muddy water into the filter.

What happens

The water that runs out of the filter is cleaner than the water poured in because the filter traps a lot of the dirt. The filters at a waterworks are very thick and make water much cleaner. Then the water has special chemicals added to it, to kill any germs that are left.

Muddy water

Flower-pot-filter

The water runs out through the hole in the bottom of the flower-pot-filter

Cleaner, filtered water

Bottle Volcano

Have you ever noticed that the first few sips of a hot drink always seem much hotter than the rest of the drink at the bottom of the cup? This simple experiment with water shows you in a dramatic way exactly what happens when you mix hot liquids and cold liquids together.

You will need

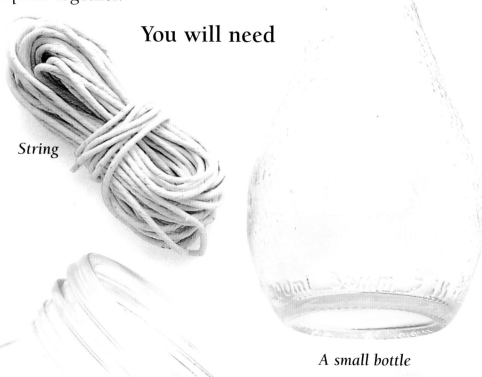

String

A small bottle

Red food colouring or ink

A large glass jar

EQUIPMENT

Scissors

Paintbrush

Setting up the volcano

1 Cut a piece of string about 30 cm long. Tie one end of it firmly around the neck of the bottle, leaving the other end free.

2 Tie the other end of the string to the piece tied around the neck of the bottle, to make a loop of string for a handle.

3 Fill the large jar with cold water from a tap or jug. Don't fill it right to the top, as you need space to lower the bottle into it.

4 Fill the small bottle right up to the top with hot water. Stir in enough drops of food colouring to turn the water bright red.

5 Hold the bottle by the string handle and lower it gently into the jar of cold water, being careful to keep it level.

VOLCANO IN A JAR

As you lower the small bottle into the jar of cold water, the hot water shoots up into the cold water like a volcano. Soon all the hot water will rise to the top of the jar.

Why hot air rises

When water is heated, it expands (takes up more space). This makes the hot water lighter than cold water, so it rises to the surface of the cold water.

ON THE LEVEL

No two liquids are the same. Have you ever wondered why cream floats on top of milk, or why salad dressing separates into different layers? And did you know that some objects will sink in water but float on another liquid? Do this experiment and you can create a colourful giant cocktail and find out some fascinating things about different liquids at the same time.

You will need

Vegetable oil

Golden syrup

EQUIPMENT

Large spoon

Jug

Nuts

Plastic toys

Water coloured with ink or food colouring

Small metal objects

Small tomatoes

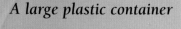

A large plastic container

Dried pasta

Grapes

10

What to do

1 Carefully pour golden syrup into the container over the back of the spoon, until the container is a quarter full.

2 Slowly pour the same amount of vegetable oil into the container. Then add the same amount again of coloured water.

3 Wait until the liquids have settled into layers. Then gently drop different objects into the container to see what floats.

LIQUID COCKTAIL

The liquids separate into three layers, with the syrup on the bottom, the water above that, and the oil on top of the water. Liquids do this because some of them are lighter, or less dense, than others. A lighter liquid will float on top of a heavier, or more dense, liquid.

Floaters and sinkers

Some of the objects you drop into the container will sink. Others will float at different levels depending on how heavy they are. Objects float best in dense liquids as these support their weight.

11

SPLITTING COLOURS

Many of the inks and dyes that are used to colour things are really mixtures of several different coloured chemicals or *pigments*. The two experiments here show you how to separate the different coloured pigments in felt-tip pens and the food colouring used in sweets.

You will need

EQUIPMENT

Glass or jam jar   *Jug of water*

Scissors

Saucers

White blotting paper

Coloured felt-tip pens

Half a teaspoon of salt

Coloured chocolate sweets

Felt-tip pen test

1 Cut out a rectangle of blotting paper big enough to roll into a tube that you can slide into the glass you are going to use.

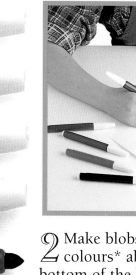

2 Make blobs of different colours* about 4 cm from the bottom of the blotting paper with the felt-tip pens.

3 Pour a little water into the glass and stir in the salt. Roll the blotting paper into a tube and stand it in the glass.

* Dark colours are the most interesting colours to test.

Sweet test

1 Choose three colours to test. Put five or six sweets the same colour in each saucer. Add a few drops of water to them.

2 Turn the sweets over and stir them round a little, so that most of the colour runs off them and colours the water.

3 Cut three strips of blotting paper. Lay a strip into each of the saucers as shown, with one end in the coloured water.

FELT-TIP PEN TEST

As the water rises up the blotting paper, it dissolves the pigments in the ink blots and carries them up with it. The different pigments move up the paper at different speeds, so they separate and you can see bands of different colours.

SWEET TEST

The pigments used on the sweets are absorbed by the blotting paper in the same way as the pigments in the felt-tip pens. As they move up the blotting paper, they separate. Some of the colours only contain one pigment.

13

MAGIC MAGNETS

Magnets have special powers that seem to be magic. Their power is called magnetism, and it can move certain objects around without even touching them. Below you can find out more about your magnet, then use its powers to do some exciting tricks.

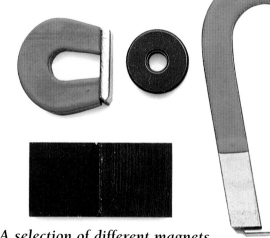

You will need

Snake pattern

A selection of different magnets

A variety of small household objects and steel paper-clips

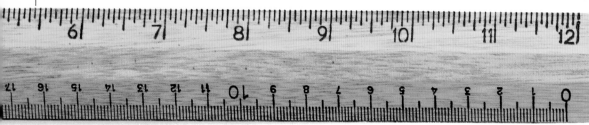

A ruler

Cotton thread

Magnetic attraction

Pieces of coloured felt

Glue

Sticky tape

EQUIPMENT

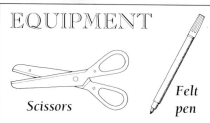

Scissors

Felt pen

Hold a magnet close to each of the objects you have collected. Which objects does the magnet pick up? What are they made of?

Making the snake

1 Trace the snake pattern on the opposite page, then cut it out in felt. Decorate your snake with small pieces of coloured felt.

2 Give the snake felt eyes and a tongue. Tie a short piece of thread to a paper-clip. Slide the paper-clip on to the snake's head.

3 Tape a magnet to one end of the ruler. Tape the thread from the snake firmly to the table, as shown.

It's magnetic magic!

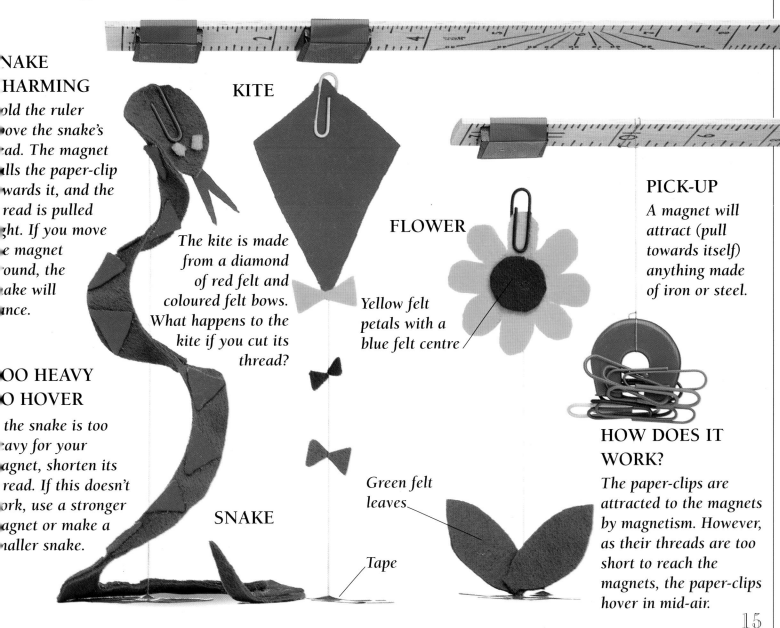

SNAKE CHARMING

Hold the ruler above the snake's head. The magnet pulls the paper-clip towards it, and the thread is pulled tight. If you move the magnet round, the snake will dance.

KITE

The kite is made from a diamond of red felt and coloured felt bows. What happens to the kite if you cut its thread?

FLOWER

Yellow felt petals with a blue felt centre

Green felt leaves

Tape

SNAKE

TOO HEAVY TO HOVER

If the snake is too heavy for your magnet, shorten its thread. If this doesn't work, use a stronger magnet or make a smaller snake.

PICK-UP

A magnet will attract (pull towards itself) anything made of iron or steel.

HOW DOES IT WORK?

The paper-clips are attracted to the magnets by magnetism. However, as their threads are too short to reach the magnets, the paper-clips hover in mid-air.

15

MAGNETIC FIELDS

A magnet's invisible powers are contained within its 'magnetic field'. You can see the pattern of a magnetic field by putting iron filings near a magnet. Iron filings usually leap towards a magnet, but if you put them in sticky syrup, they will form magnetic patterns very slowly. Stir up the filings in the syrup, every time you use the mixture.

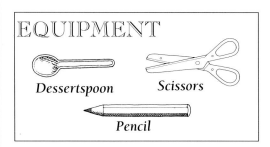

EQUIPMENT

Dessertspoon

Scissors

Pencil

You will need

A selection of different magnets

Some string

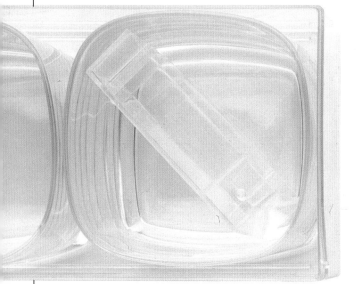

Clear plastic tubs or glass containers

Iron filings

Iron filings

Golden syrup

Plastic wrap

Making the mixture

Sprinkle a dessertspoonful of iron filings into the syrup. Stir gently until the iron filings are evenly mixed into the syrup.

Magnetic patterns

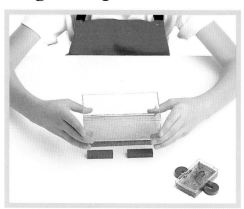

Pour some mixture into each tub. Place magnets underneath or at the sides of the tubs, then watch as the magnetic fields appear.

3-D fields

Fill a glass with mixture. Cover a bar magnet in plastic wrap, and tie it to a pencil with string. Hang the magnet in the middle of the glass.

Fields of filings

Each magnet forms a magnetic-field-pattern. Test magnets of different shapes, sizes, and strengths, and compare the fields they make. Then look at the fields you can produce when you put two or more magnets near each other. Here are some of the patterns we found.

17

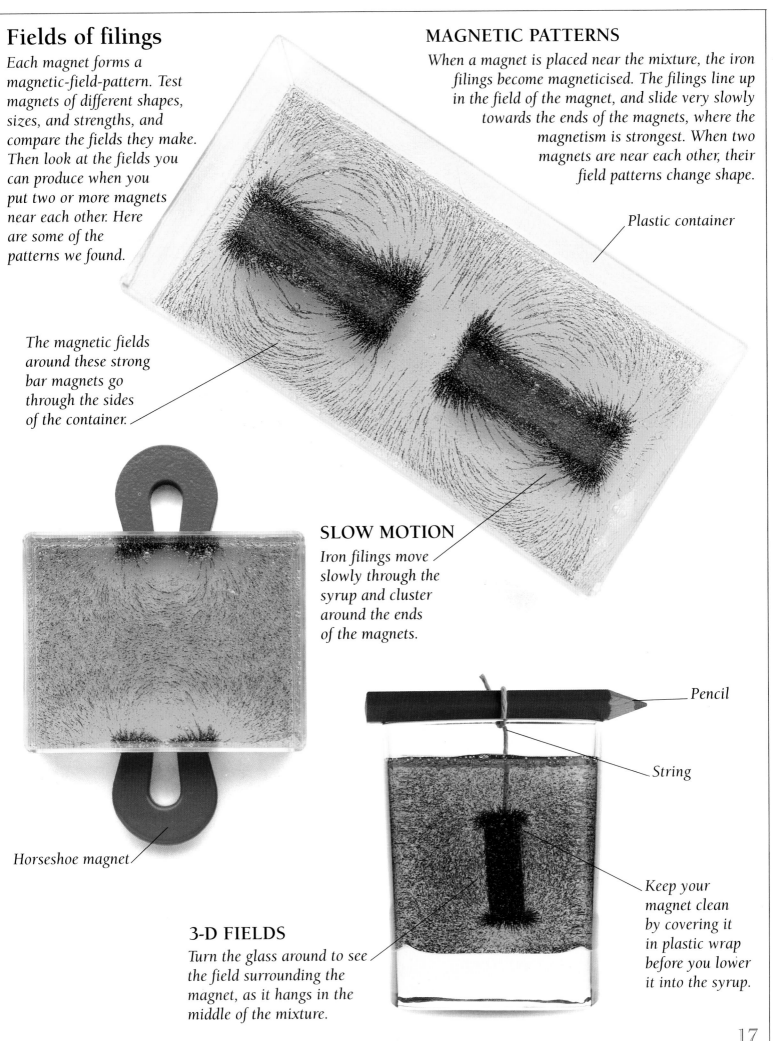

MAGNETIC PATTERNS

When a magnet is placed near the mixture, the iron filings become magneticised. The filings line up in the field of the magnet, and slide very slowly towards the ends of the magnets, where the magnetism is strongest. When two magnets are near each other, their field patterns change shape.

Plastic container

The magnetic fields around these strong bar magnets go through the sides of the container.

SLOW MOTION

Iron filings move slowly through the syrup and cluster around the ends of the magnets.

Pencil

String

Keep your magnet clean by covering it in plastic wrap before you lower it into the syrup.

Horseshoe magnet

3-D FIELDS

Turn the glass around to see the field surrounding the magnet, as it hangs in the middle of the mixture.

POLES APART

Every magnet has a north pole and a south pole, like the Earth. These poles are the two opposite ends, or sides, of a magnet, where its powers are strongest. You can find out more about magnetic poles, how to identify them and why magnets behave oddly when they are together, in the experiments below. Opposite you can see how to make your own magnets, as well as an amazing turtle compass that really works.

Poster paint

A bottle top

EQUIPMENT

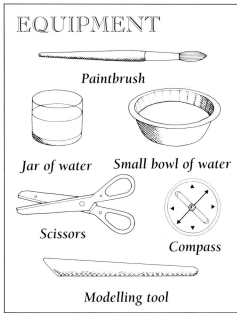

Paintbrush

Jar of water   *Small bowl of water*

Scissors

Compass

Modelling tool

Wooden skewers

A horseshoe magnet   **You will need**   *A steel needle*

Coloured modelling clay

Strong bar magnets   *Ring magnets*

North or south pole?

Hang a bar magnet above the compass, as shown*. When it stops moving, the end pointing north is the magnet's north pole.

Pole position

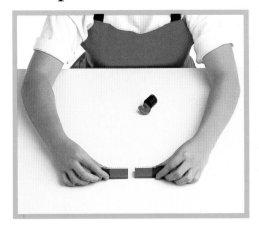

Try pushing the north poles, then the south poles of two magnets together. What happens? Next, try a north and a south pole together.

Making the lion

Paint some skewers, cut them in half, and stick them in some clay around a bar magnet. Model a clay lion. Sit it on another bar magnet.

Making the clown

Stick three skewers into some clay. Put some ring magnets on to the skewers. Model a clown from clay, and stick it on the top magnet.

18

* The magnet will affect the compass needle if it is too close.

Turtle compass

1 Stroke a needle, 30 times from its point to its eye, with the south pole of a magnet. Make a light, flat turtle from clay.

2 Push the turtle on to the open end of the bottle top. Stick the needle point firmly into the turtle's tail, directly opposite its head.

TURTLE COMPASS

The needle becomes a magnet when it is stroked by a magnet. As it floats in the bowl, it is affected by the Earth's magnetic field. The turtle's head points to the north and the eye of the needle in its tail points south.

BOUNCING CLOWN

The clown bounces on the invisible magnetic fields of the magnets.

The clown's body is hollow so that it is light enough to bounce on the magnets.

OPPOSITES ATTRACT…

The north pole of one magnet and the south pole of another magnet attract (pull towards) each other, and the magnets snap together.

Modelling clay clown

…LIKE POLES REPEL

Two north poles or two south poles together, repel (push away from) each other, so the magnets 'float' one above the other.

Modelling clay base

Skewer cage bars

The top magnet will not float if the lion is too heavy.

Modelling clay lion

South pole

South pole

North pole

North pole

LEVITATING LION

Put the magnet with the lion in the cage, with like poles sitting on top of each other. The magnets repel each other, making the top magnet float. Try turning the top magnet, or removing the cage bars.

KITCHEN CHEMISTRY

You don't need special powders and test tubes to be a chemist. Everything around you is made of chemicals, and you can do all kinds of interesting tests on things around the kitchen. Here and on the next three pages you can find out how to test things to see if they are acid or alkaline.

Blotting paper

Half a lemon

You will need

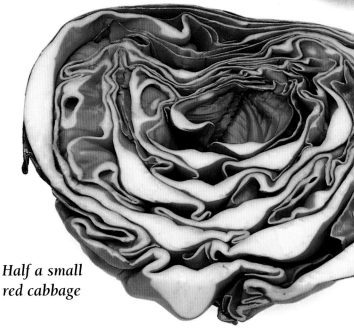

Bicarbonate of soda

Water

Half a small red cabbage

The acid test

1 Chop up the cabbage and put it in a bowl. Pour hot water over it and leave it to soak until the water turns purple.

2 Hold the sieve over the jug. Pour the cabbage water into the jug through the sieve, so that the cabbage stays in the sieve.

3 Pour a little purple cabbage water into several of the small jars. Label one jar *Control* and put it to one side.

20

Other things to test

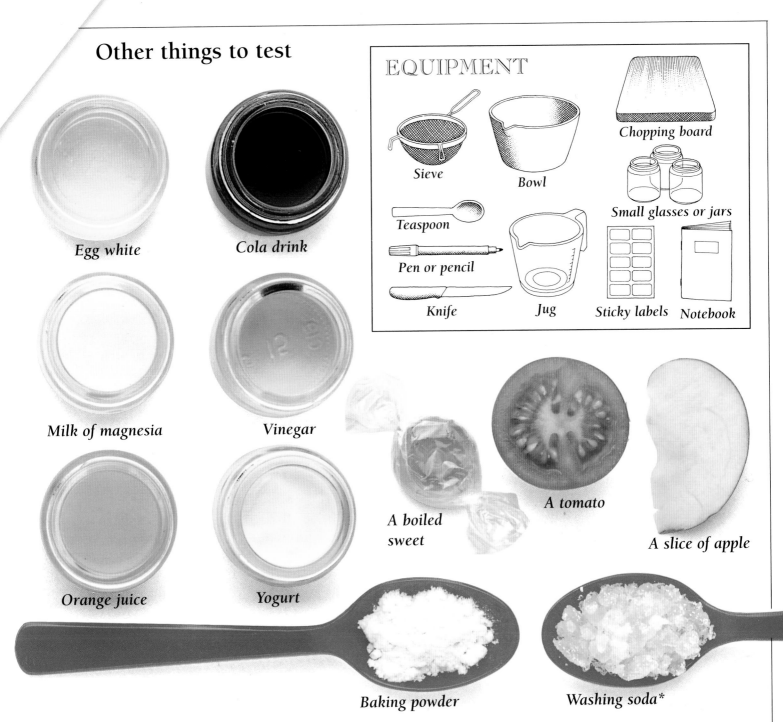

EQUIPMENT

Sieve

Bowl

Chopping board

Teaspoon

Pen or pencil

Knife

Jug

Sticky labels

Notebook

Small glasses or jars

Egg white

Cola drink

Milk of magnesia

Vinegar

A boiled sweet

A tomato

A slice of apple

Orange juice

Yogurt

Baking powder

Washing soda*

4 Pour a few drops of lemon juice into one of the other jars of purple cabbage water. Label the jar *Lemon juice*.

5 Mix a teaspoon of bicarbonate of soda with a little water. Stir it into a jar of purple water. Label it *Bicarbonate of soda*.

6 Do the same with all the other things you want to test. Label every jar to say what is in it as you do each test.

* Wash your hands after touching washing soda.

MAGIC POTIONS

Changing colour

1 Squeeze a little lemon juice into two jars. Mix two teaspoons of bicarbonate of soda with water in a third jar.

2 Add some purple cabbage water to the two jars of lemon juice. The lemon juice should turn pink. Label one jar *Control*.

3 Add the bicarbonate of soda to the pink lemon juice, drop by drop. What happens to the colour of the lemon juice?

THE ACID TEST

Alkalis

If the cabbage water turns blue or green, as it does with bicarbonate of soda, the thing you have tested is an alkali.

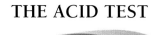
Lemon

Bicarbonate of soda

Control jar
You keep the Control jar to compare with the tests you do.

Purple water with lemon juice added to it

Purple water with a sweet added to it

Acids
If the purple cabbage water turns pink, as with the lemon juice, the thing you have tested is acid.

Purple water with bicarbonate of soda added to it

Other things to test

1 Cut a piece of blotting paper into small strips about 1.5 cm wide. Cut a lot of strips so that you can test several liquids.

2 Dip the strips of blotting paper into purple cabbage water, then lay them on a saucer to dry. This may take a few hours.

3 Dip a strip of paper into each liquid you want to test. Try lemon juice, then bicarbonate of soda mixed with water.

CHANGING COLOUR

As you add the bicarbonate of soda (an alkali) to the lemon juice (an acid), the pink water turns purple. This shows that the liquid is no longer acid.

Lemon juice

Purple water with lemon juice added to it

Bicarbonate of soda

Pink water with bicarbonate of soda added to it

Strips of indicator paper

MAKING INDICATOR PAPER

Scientists use indicator paper to test liquids to see if they are acid or alkaline. You can make your own. When you dip indicator paper into an acid, it turns pink. When you dip it into an alkali, it turns blue or green.

23

DIRTY WATER TEST

Have you ever wondered where all your water comes from? The fresh water that pours out of our taps comes from rivers, lakes, streams, reservoirs, and from deep beneath the ground. All living things need clean water – but the Earth is like a sponge and soaks up anything liquid that is dumped on the ground or into the rivers. This simple experiment shows you what happens when pollutants get into the water system.

A stick of celery

EQUIPMENT

3 glass jars

Knife

You will need

White flowers

Coloured ink or food colouring

A jug of water

What to do

1 Pour about 2 cm of food colouring or ink into each glass. Add the same amount again of water to each glass.

2 Trim the flower and celery stems. Stand the celery and flowers in coloured water and leave them for a few hours.

HOW YOU CAN HELP

• Encourage your family to use ecological washing powders and washing-up liquid.
• Avoid using chemical fertilisers and pesticides in the garden.
• Tell your parents never to pour DIY chemicals or car oil down the drain.

DIRTY WATER

The plants absorb the coloured water. The colouring acts like pollution.

As the plants drink the water, they drink up any pollution that is in it. This happens to any person or animal that drinks polluted water.

WATER POLLUTION

Factory wastes and the run-off from chemicals cause water pollution. But a lot of pollution also starts at home.

FLYING PAPER

How do aeroplanes fly? Launch a piece of paper into the air and it will just swoop down to the ground. But if you make a plane with the piece of paper, it will fly really well. Here and on the next three pages you can find out how to make an amazing superglider and helicopter. They are not only fun to make and play with, but will also teach you a lot about how things fly.

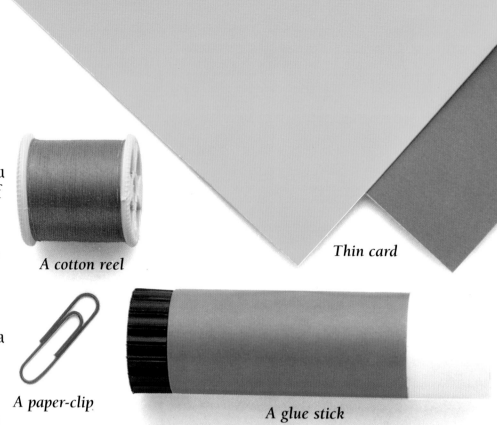

A cotton reel

Thin card

A paper-clip

A glue stick

You will need

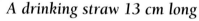

A drinking straw 13 cm long

Tracing paper

A small lump of modelling clay

String

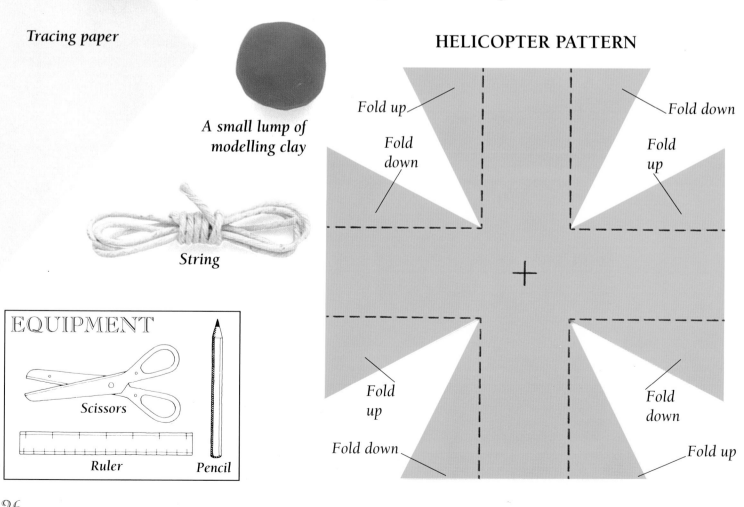

EQUIPMENT

Scissors

Ruler

Pencil

HELICOPTER PATTERN

Fold up

Fold down

Fold down

Fold up

Fold up

Fold down

Fold down

Fold up

SUPERGLIDER PATTERN

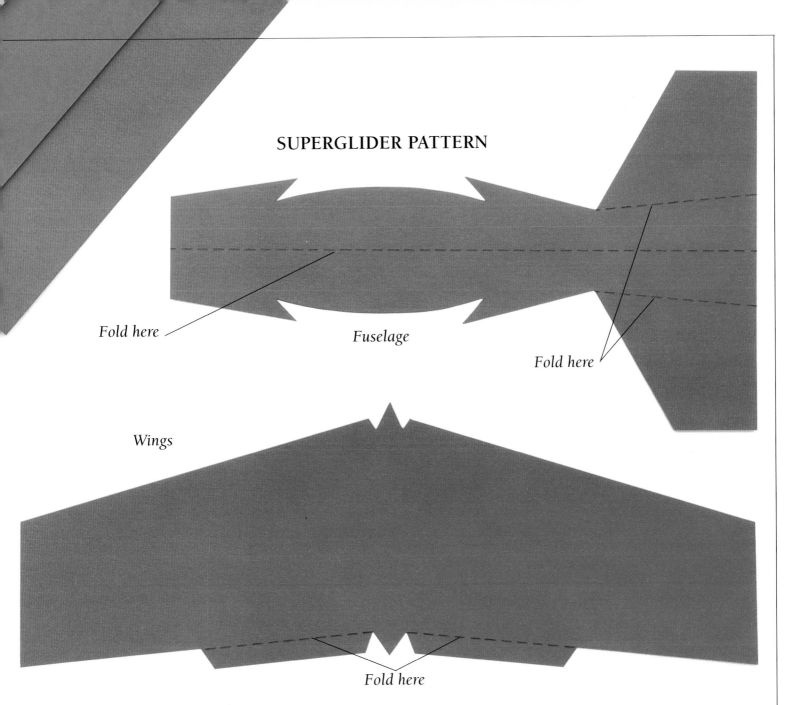

Fold here

Fuselage

Fold here

Wings

Fold here

Making the superglider

1 Trace the outlines of the two superglider pattern pieces on to tracing paper. Trace along the fold lines using dotted lines.

2 Turn the tracing paper over. Lay it on the card and scribble over the lines you have traced, to transfer the pattern to the card.

3 Cut the wings and fuselage out of the card. Score along the fold lines, using your ruler and the point of your scissors*.

This helps to make the folds sharper.

FLYING HIGH
Superglider (continued)

4 Fold the fuselage in half along the fold line, then open it out again. Fold down the two tail fins and the two wing flaps.

5 Slot the back of the wings into the back notches on the fuselage. Slot the front of the wings into the front two notches.

6 Put the paper-clip on the nose of the aeroplane. Fold a piece of modelling clay around the paper-clip, to act as a weight.

Making the helicopter

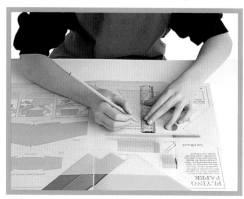

1 Trace the pattern for the helicopter rotor on to tracing paper. Trace the fold lines, using dotted lines.

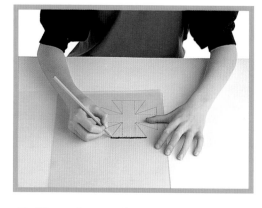

2 Turn the tracing paper over. Lay it on the card and scribble over the lines you have traced, to transfer the pattern to the card.

3 Cut the helicopter rotor out of the card. Score along the fold lines, using your ruler and the point of your scissors.

4 Each rotor blade has two fold lines. Fold one side of each rotor blade up and the other side down, along the fold lines.

5 Make a hole in the middle of the rotor. Spread glue around one end of the straw. Push the straw through the hole in the rotor.

6 Make a loop in one end of the string. Wind string anti-clockwise over the loop around the straw beneath the rotor.

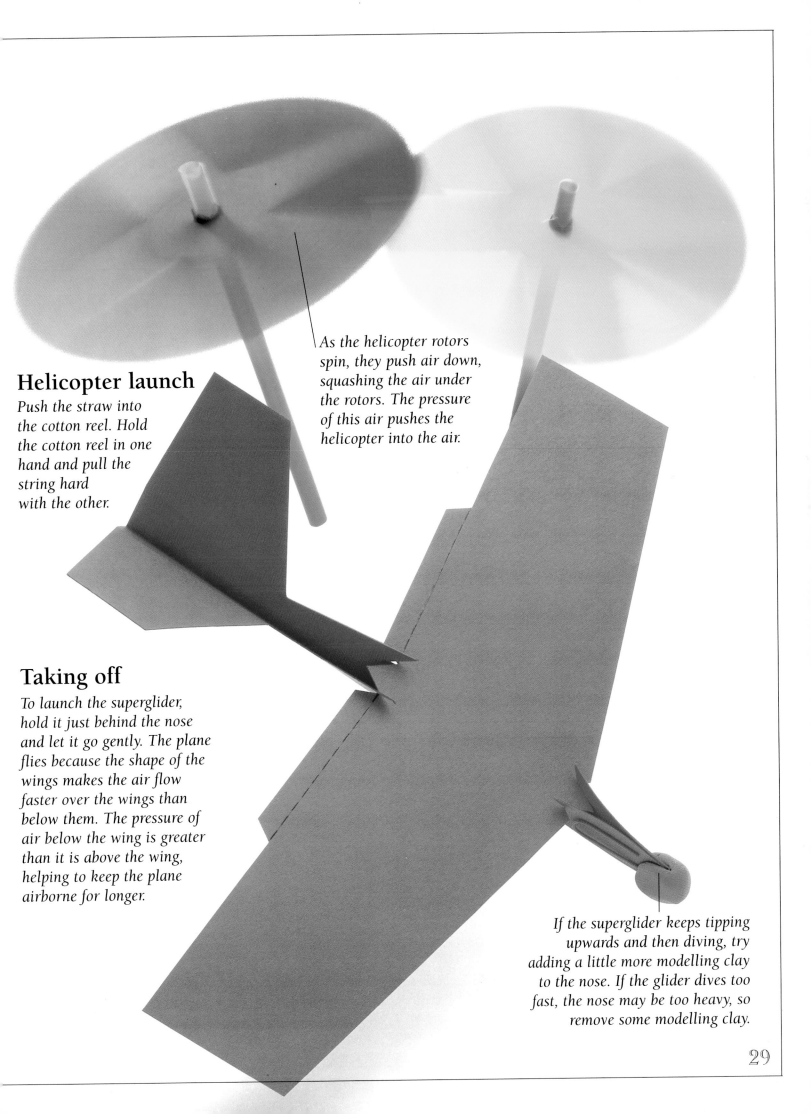

Helicopter launch

Push the straw into the cotton reel. Hold the cotton reel in one hand and pull the string hard with the other.

As the helicopter rotors spin, they push air down, squashing the air under the rotors. The pressure of this air pushes the helicopter into the air.

Taking off

To launch the superglider, hold it just behind the nose and let it go gently. The plane flies because the shape of the wings makes the air flow faster over the wings than below them. The pressure of air below the wing is greater than it is above the wing, helping to keep the plane airborne for longer.

If the superglider keeps tipping upwards and then diving, try adding a little more modelling clay to the nose. If the glider dives too fast, the nose may be too heavy, so remove some modelling clay.

VANISHING COLOURS

Light looks white, but it is really made of rainbow colours. Make this simple multi-coloured wheel and you will be able to make colours disappear, then appear again, as if by magic. Where do the colours go and why? Spin the wheel, then read about what happens at the bottom of the page opposite.

You will need

Thin card

A short, sharp pencil

A glue stick

Coloured paper (red, orange, yellow, green, blue, and purple)

Tracing paper

EQUIPMENT

Sharp pencil

Scissors

Pair of compasses

Ruler

Making the colour wheel

1 Open the compasses to 5 cm and draw a circle on the card. Mark six points, 5 cm apart, around the circle with the compasses.

2 Join each pair of opposite points together, so the three lines cross in the centre of the circle. Cut out the circle.

3 Trace a segment of the circle. Glue it on to card and cut it out. Draw round the shape on each colour of paper and cut it out.

4 Glue the pieces of coloured paper to the circle of card in this order: red, orange, yellow, green, blue, and purple.

5 Punch a hole in the centre of the circle with the tip of the scissors. Push the pencil through the hole, as shown.

SPINNING COLOURS

Spin the colour wheel fast and watch what happens. Which colour or colours can you see? When the wheel spins fast, your eyes and brain working together cannot see each colour separately, so the colours blur together to make a different colour.

As the colour wheel slows down, the blurring lessens, and your eyes and brain can pick out the different colours again. Try making other wheels in just two or three colours. Do you always see the same colour when you spin them?